CONTENTS

First **Impressions**   2

Making **Friends**   4

Earning **Respect**   6

Being **Polite**   8

General **Behaviour**   10

> **First impressions will always stay,
> Follow Mac Manners, he knows the way.**

When meeting people here and there,
Don't forget, it's rude to stare.
You must only point at objects or things,
Never at people, not even a King!

When answering the phone, your number you should say,
Then the caller knows that they have connected okay.
Just answering 'Hello' is not much of a clue,
For the caller to know who they are speaking to.

If you are bored don't let it show,
It can be hurtful to let others know.
Answer when spoken to with a nice reply,
Or others may think you are sulky or shy.

If you've been to a party or weekend away,
Always thank your host for a wonderful stay.
But if you've left before seeing your host,
Then send your thanks by phone or post.

> **Mac Manners makes new friends easily,
> He just follows these rules, one, two, three.**

When visitors arrive and you are seated,
Make sure you stand up before they are greeted,
When you are saying goodbye leap to your feet,
It is hard to embrace when still in your seat.

A friend of yours may feel out in the cold,
Unless introduced to others young or old,
This rule applies wherever you should meet,
Out shopping, playing or just in the street.

Make new friends but keep the old,
One is silver the other is gold.
Ask them to join you and your friends,
Start a new friendship before it ends.

When introduced to someone new,
Hold out your hand and say 'How do you do?'
If someone should do this to you,
Reply, 'I'm fine thanks, How are you?'

> **Respect for others earns respect for you,
> Mac Manners will show you just what to do.**

When playing with toys learn to share,
Being selfish is just not fair.
As you grow up you will learn,
What you give you gain in return.

Some think it's strong to bully and shout,
But that is not what life's all about.
If you are pleasant and stop being blue,
Then others will always be nice to you.

Swearing and cursing isn't so tough,
It shows that you haven't learnt enough.
Find the correct word to say what you mean,
This will ensure that your language is clean.

If plans have changed, then let your friends know,
Or they shall be thinking when will you show?
And don't forget friendships could go astray,
If you are always late turning up to play.

> **Mac Manners knows that being polite is cool,
> If you don't know the ropes then it's back to school**

When boys walk on the outside, they must try,
To shield the girls from danger passing by.
The girl goes first unless climbing the stairs,
This saves her showing you her underwear.

Stand to the side, let elders pass,
This will take you to the top of the class.
The day will come when you may need advice,
So don't cheek your elders, try to be nice.

Join the back of the queue, do not push through,
Would you like others to do this to you?
If you need to pass when someone's in the way,
'Excuse me please', is all you need say.

For those less able hold open the door,
Or those with arms full of shopping galore.
Give up your seat to the frail or the old,
This is not being cissy, but strong and bold.

> **What you say and do can reveal so much,
> Let Mac Manners show you the Golden touch.**

Sneezing and coughing spread germs North and South,
Unless you cover your nose and your mouth.
A yawn once started is very hard to hide,
Cover with your hand, it shows you've tried.

Don't bite at your nails or pick yourself raw,
Wait until you are behind a closed door.
Do not interrupt on another persons' conversation,
They were talking first, so show some consideration.

If when walking down the street,
A lady you know you happen to meet,
Raise your cap and say 'Good Day',
It may be old fashioned but will make her day.

The chewing of gum may give you a thrill,
This looks ugly, so don't until,
You are on your own for just a minute,
Then you can really chew, chew, chew it!

We all wear a different colour of skin, But everyone is the same from within.